STAR WARS®
WORKBOOKS

MATHS SKILLS

FOR AGES 5–6

BY THE EDITORS OF BRAIN QUEST
CONSULTING EDITOR: DALE BLAESS

SCHOLASTIC

Scholastic Children's Books
Euston House,
24 Eversholt Street,
London NW1 1DB, UK

A division of Scholastic Ltd
London ~ New York ~ Toronto ~ Sydney ~ Auckland
Mexico City ~ New Delhi ~ Hong Kong

First published in the USA by Workman Publishing in 2014.
This edition published in the UK by Scholastic Ltd in 2015.

Workbook series design by Raquel Jaramillo
Cover illustration by Mike Sutfin
Interior illustrations by Scott Cohn

ISBN 978 1407 16280 5

Printed in the UK by Bell and Bain Ltd, Glasgow

2 4 6 8 10 9 7 5 3 1

Papers used by Scholastic Children's Books are made from woods grown in sustainable forests.

www.scholastic.co.uk

WORKBOOKS

This workbook belongs to:

_____

0

Trace the number **0**.

Now write the number **0**.

Help Chewbacca find the Wookiees in his unit.

Circle the Wookiees with the number **0**.

1

Trace the number 1.

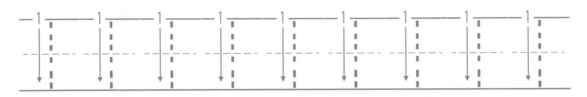

Now write the number 1.

Help the stormtroopers find the AT-AT walkers.

Colour in the AT-AT walkers with the number I.

2

Trace the number **2**.

Now write the number **2**.

Start

2 2 2 2 2 2 2 2 2 2 2 2
2
2
2
2
2
2 2 2
3
8
5 1 4 0 6 6 3 8
3
7

Help Chewbacca and Han Solo get to the *Millennium Falcon*!

Follow the number **2** from Start to End.

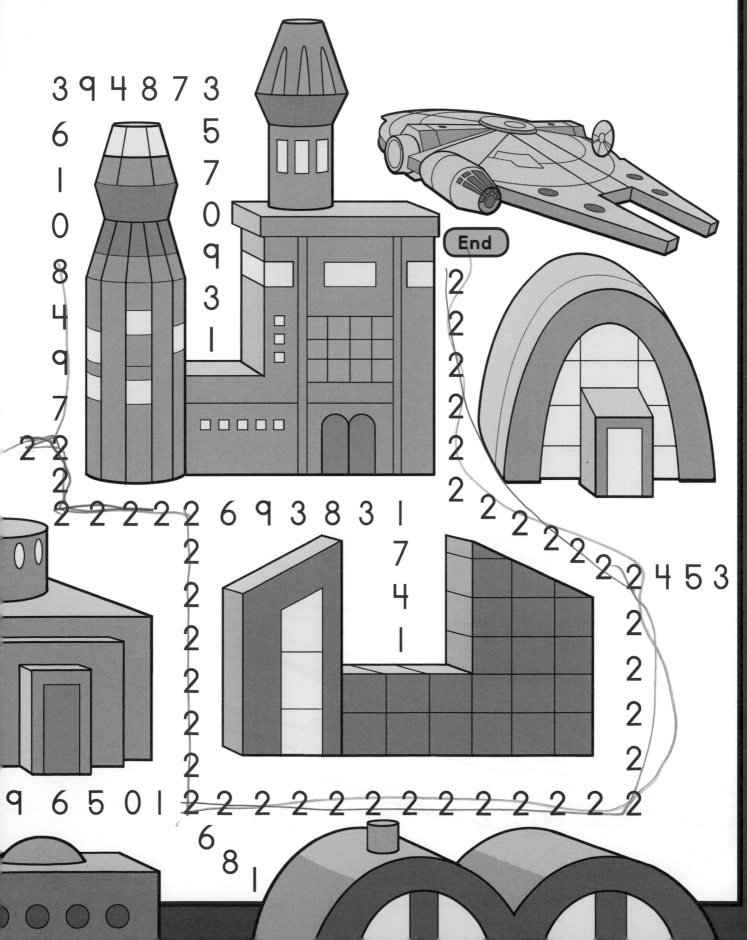

3

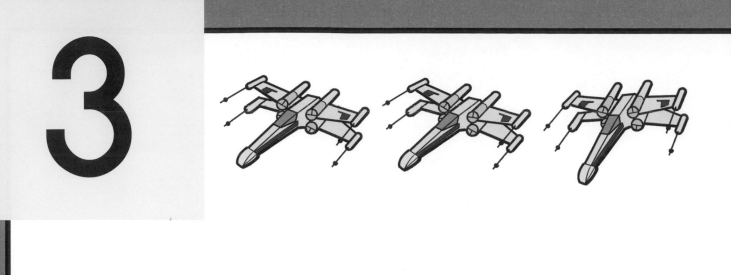

Trace the number **3**.

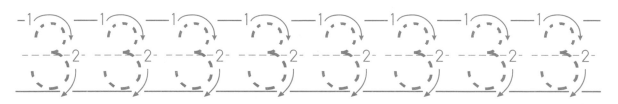

Now write the number **3**.

Help Luke Skywalker find the enemy starships in space.

Colour in the starships with the number **3**.

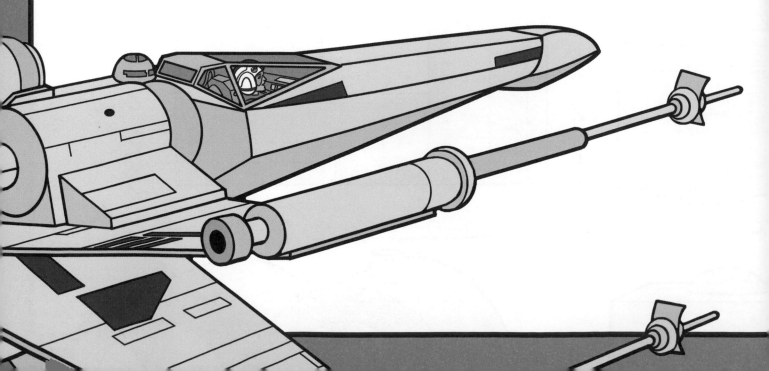

4

Trace the number **4**.

Now write the number **4**.

Which droids stay in storage locker **4**?

Circle the droids with the number **4**.

STORAGE LOCKER 4

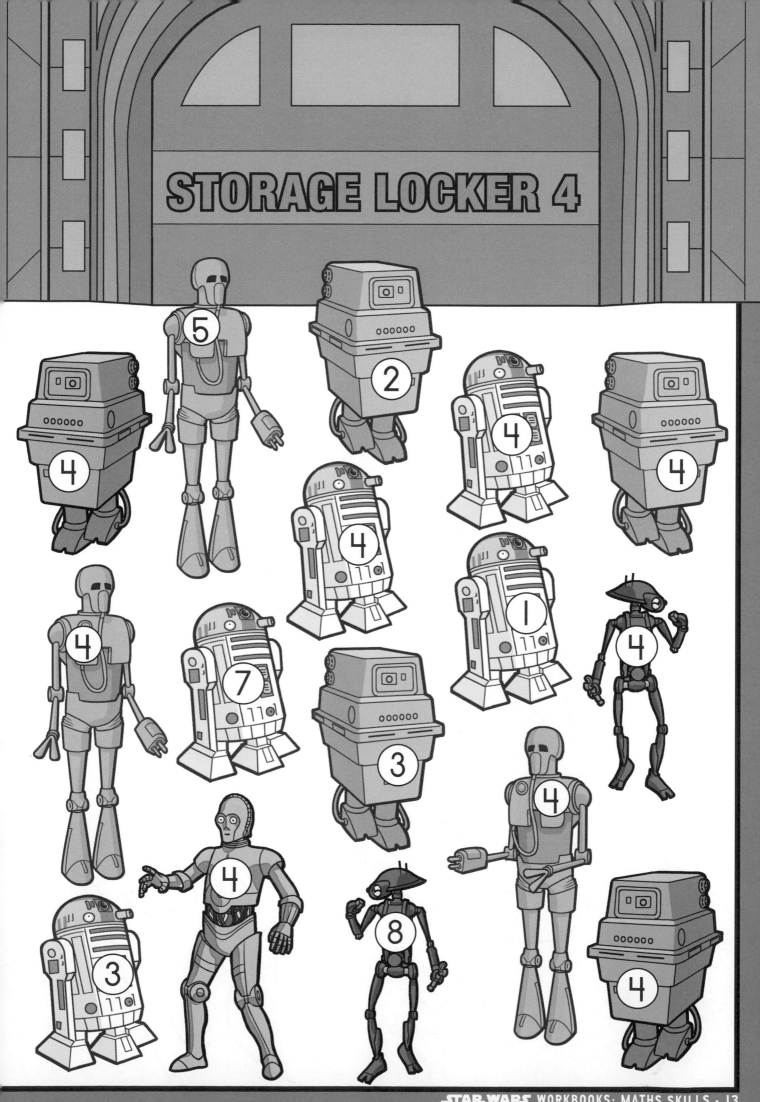

5

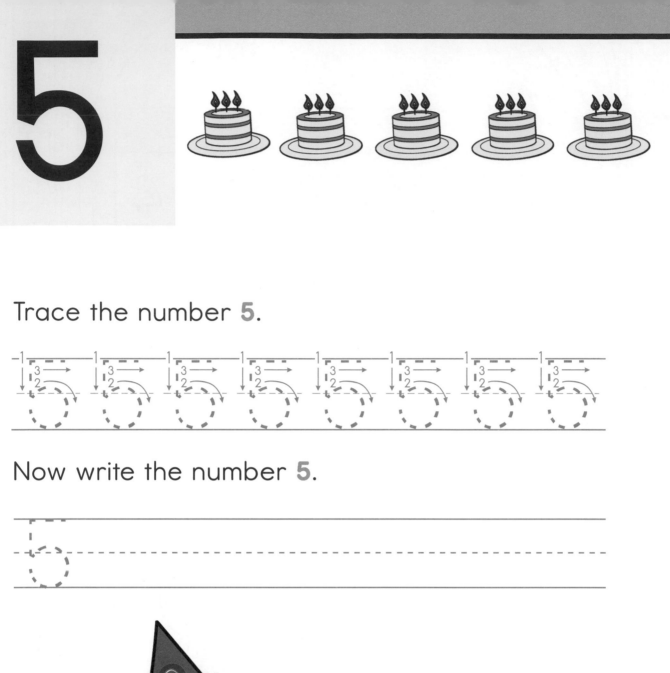

Trace the number **5**.

Now write the number **5**.

Help Jabba the Hutt celebrate his birthday!

Circle each number **5** on the cake.

6

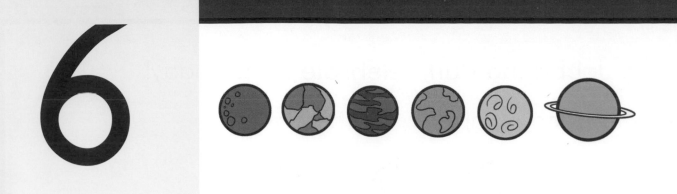

Trace the number **6**.

6 6 6 6 6 6 6 6

Now write the number **6**.

6

Darth Vader is searching the universe for Luke Skywalker.

Colour in the planets with the number **6**.

7

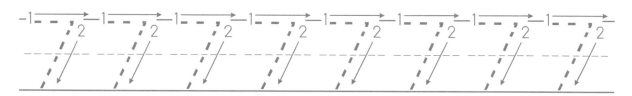

Trace the number **7**.

Now write the number **7**.

Help Anakin Skywalker win this race!

Follow the number **7** from Start to End.

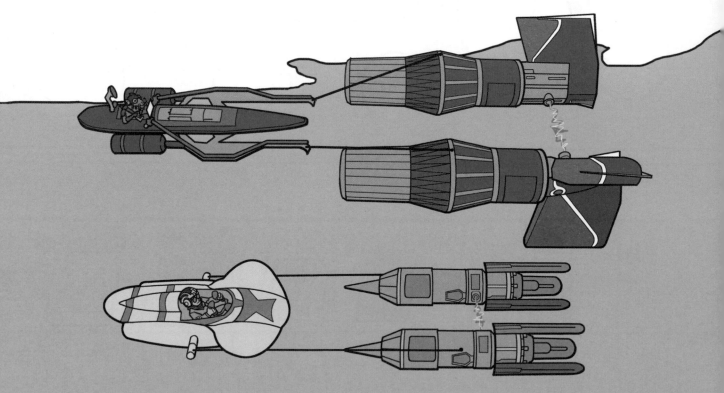

End

Start

8

Trace the number 8.

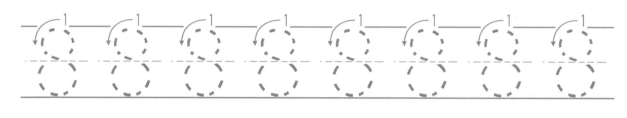

Now write the number 8.

Yoda put the number 8 on his favourite clay pots.

Circle the clay pots with the number 8.

9

Trace the number 9.

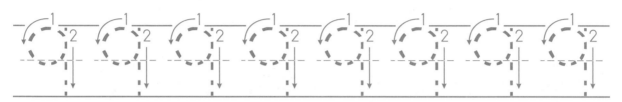

Now write the number 9.

Help the Ewok climb the tree.

Follow the number 9 from Start to End.

10

Trace the number 10.

Now write the number 10.

What are Darth Maul and
Emperor Palpatine looking at?

Colour in the spaces with the number 10.

1

5

7

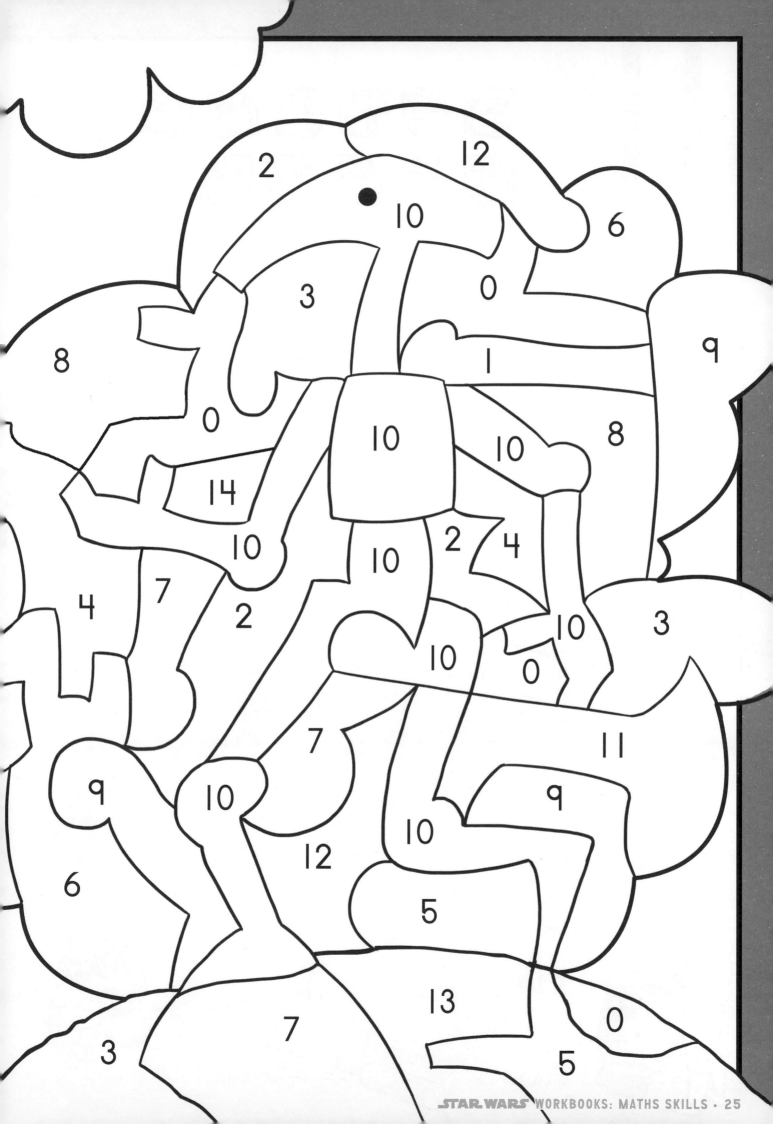

11

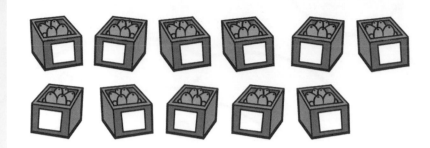

Trace the number **11**.

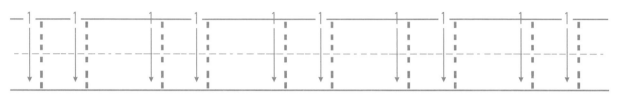

Now write the number **11**.

There are a lot of numbers at the market.

Circle each number **11**.

12

Trace the number 12.

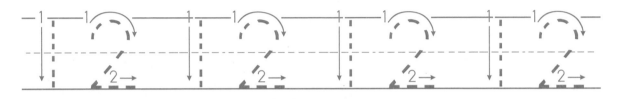

Now write the number 12.

Start

Help the tauntaun across the planet Hoth!

Follow the number **12** from

Start to End.

13

Trace the number **13**.

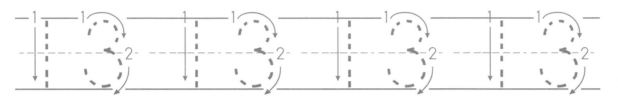

Now write the number **13**.

Help Jar Jar find the tools he dropped.

Circle the tools with the number 13.

14

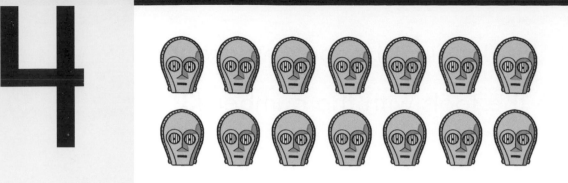

Trace the number **14**.

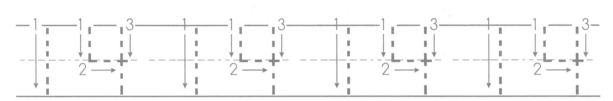

Now write the number **14**.

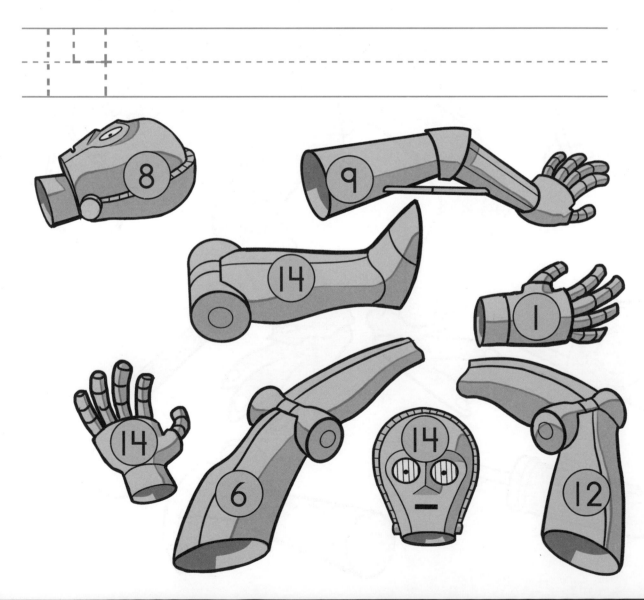

Help C-3PO find his missing parts.

Circle the parts with the number 14.

15

Trace the number 15.

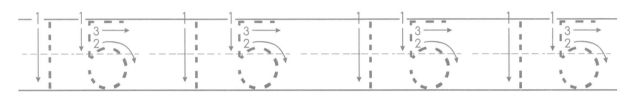

Now write the number 15.

Help Obi-Wan Kenobi find a path through the battle droids to rescue Queen Amidala!

Follow the number 15 from Start to End.

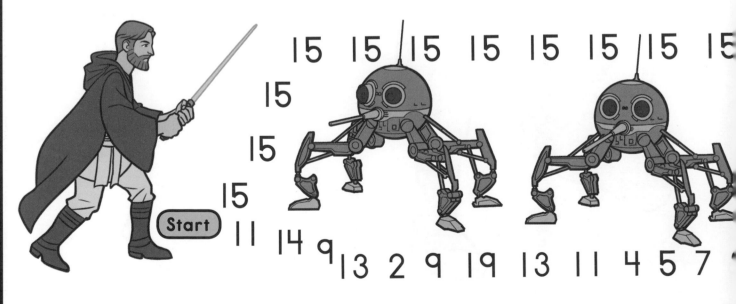

15 15 15 15 15 15 15 15

15

15

15

Start   11 14 9 13 2 9 19 13 11 4 5 7

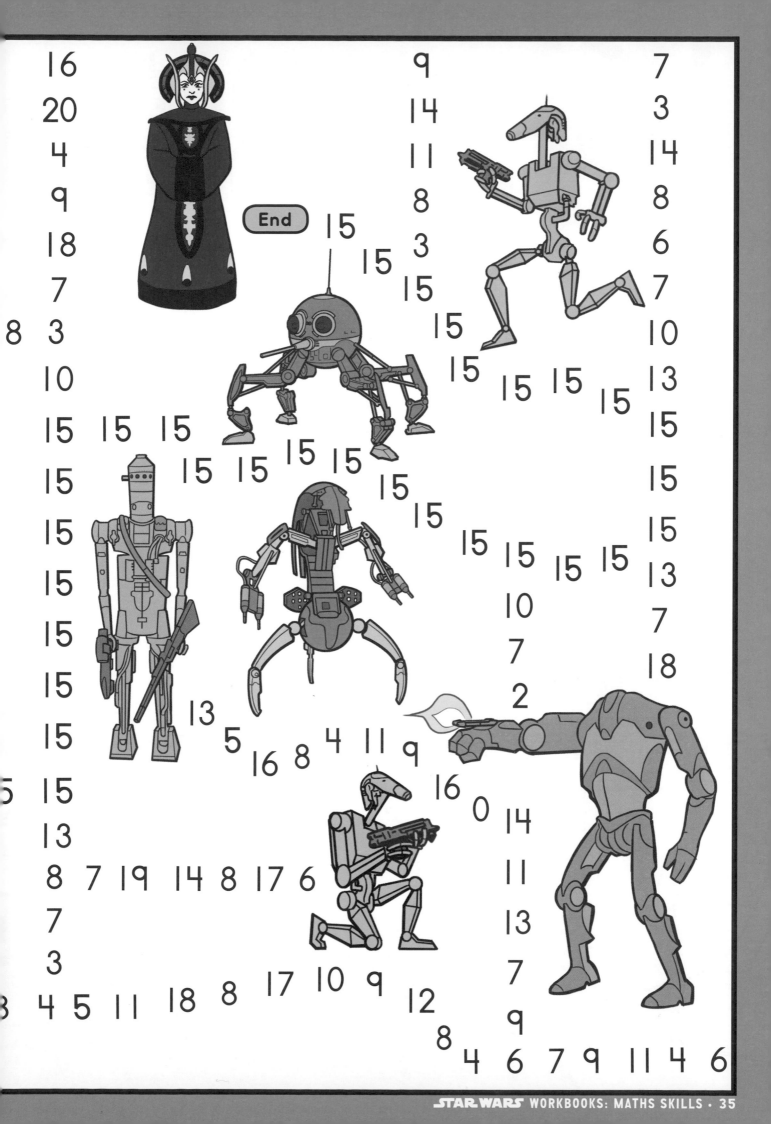

16
20
4
9
18
7
8 3
10
15 15 15
15
15 15
15 15 15
15
15
15
15
5 15
13
8 7 19 14 8 17 6
7
3
8 4 5 11 18 8 17 10 9 12

End 15
15
15 15
15 15 15
15
13

5 16 8 4 11 9 16
0 14
11
13
7
9

9
14
11
8
3
15
15
15
15 15 15
15
15 15 15 15
10
7
2

7
3
14
8
6
7
10
13
15
15
15
13
7
18

8
4 6 7 9 11 4 6

16

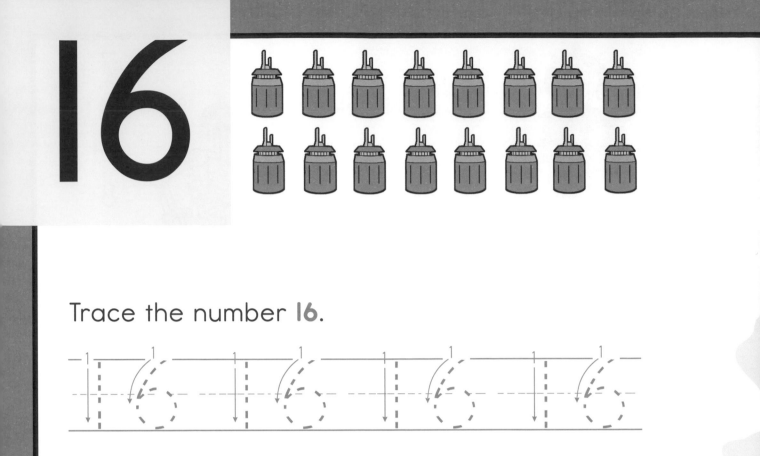

Trace the number 16.

1↓ 6 1↓ 6 1↓ 6 1↓ 6

Now write the number 16.

16

There are many numbers in Cloud City.

Colour in the buildings with the number 16.

17

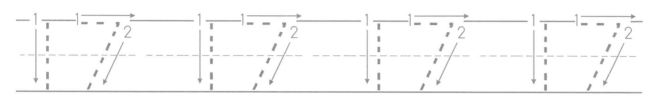

Trace the number **17**.

Now write the number **17**.

Help Boba Fett put Han Solo into his cargo hold.

Follow the number **17** from
Start to End.

Start 17 17

18

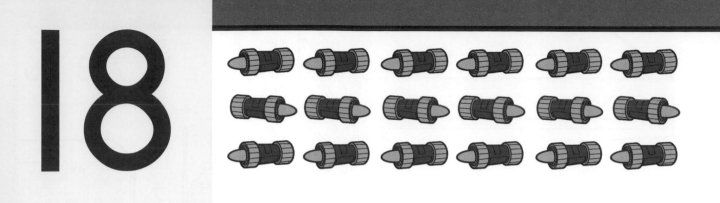

Trace the number **18**.

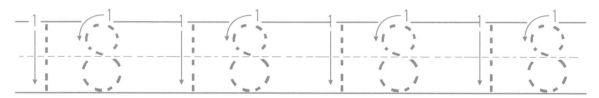

Now write the number **18**.

Help the Jedi use the Force to make objects with the number **18** float.

Circle the objects with the number **18**.

19

Trace the number 19.

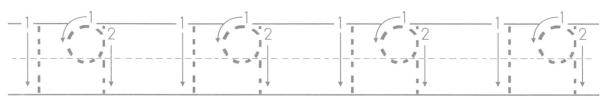

Now write the number 19.

Who is Queen Amidala talking to?

Colour in the spaces with the number 19.

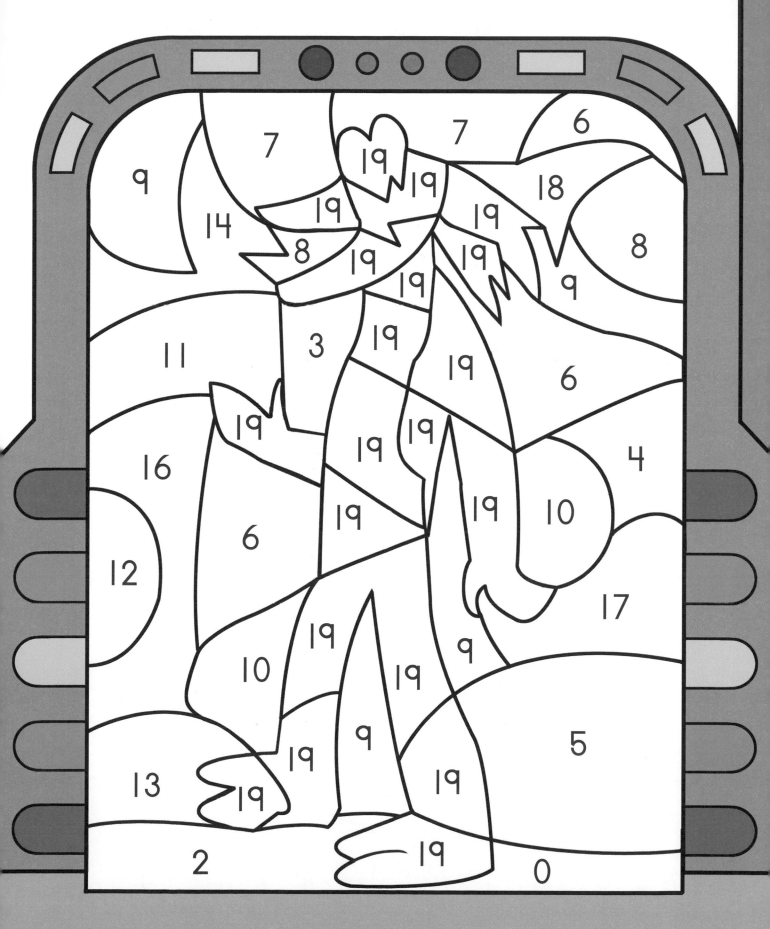

20

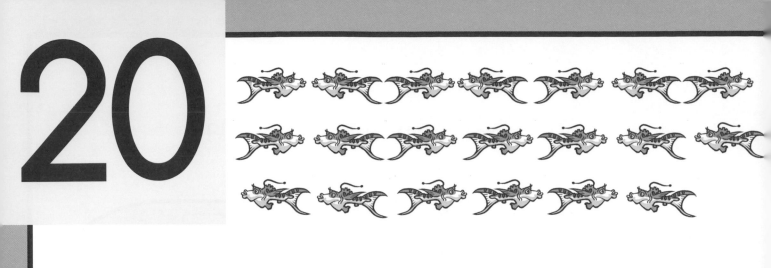

Trace the number **20**.

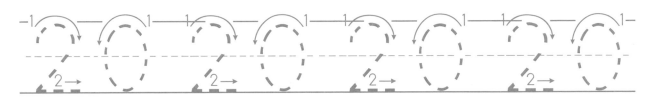

Now write the number **20**.

Help the ship reach the underwater city.

Follow the number **20** from Start to End.

Start 20 20 20

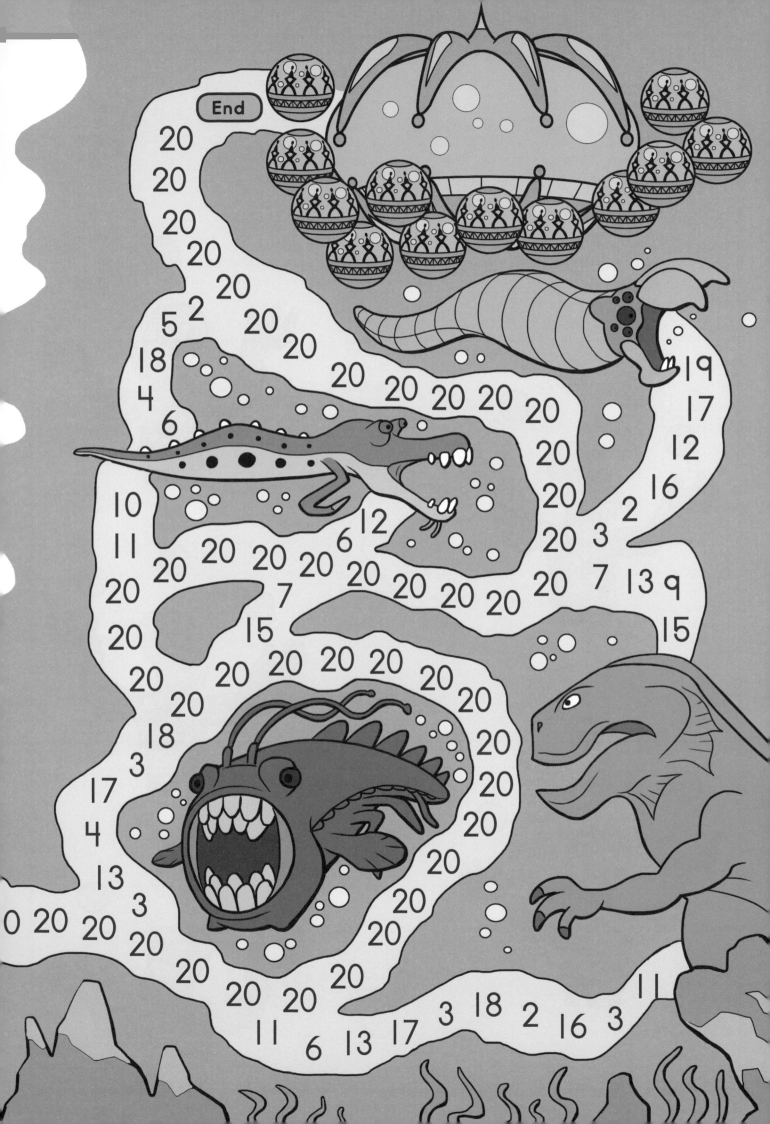

Juggle!

How many balls is Chewbacca juggling?

Draw a line to the correct number.

1

2

3

4

5

Starships!

How many Jedi starfighters are in each group?

Draw a line to the correct number.

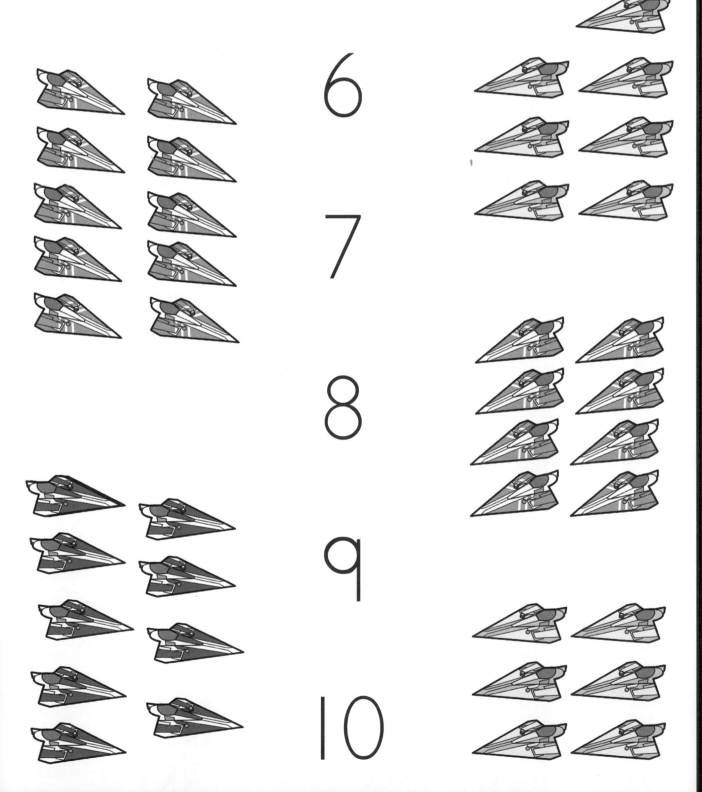

6

7

8

9

10

Creatures!

Count the creatures in each group.

Write the number on the cards next to the creatures.

rancors

reeks

nexu

wampas

acklay

dewbacks

varactyls

tauntauns

rontos

banthas

Visit Naboo!

Count how many creatures are in each group.

Write the number on the cards next to the creatures.

_____

- - - - - - - -

_____

falumpasets

_____

- - - - - - - -

_____

shaaks

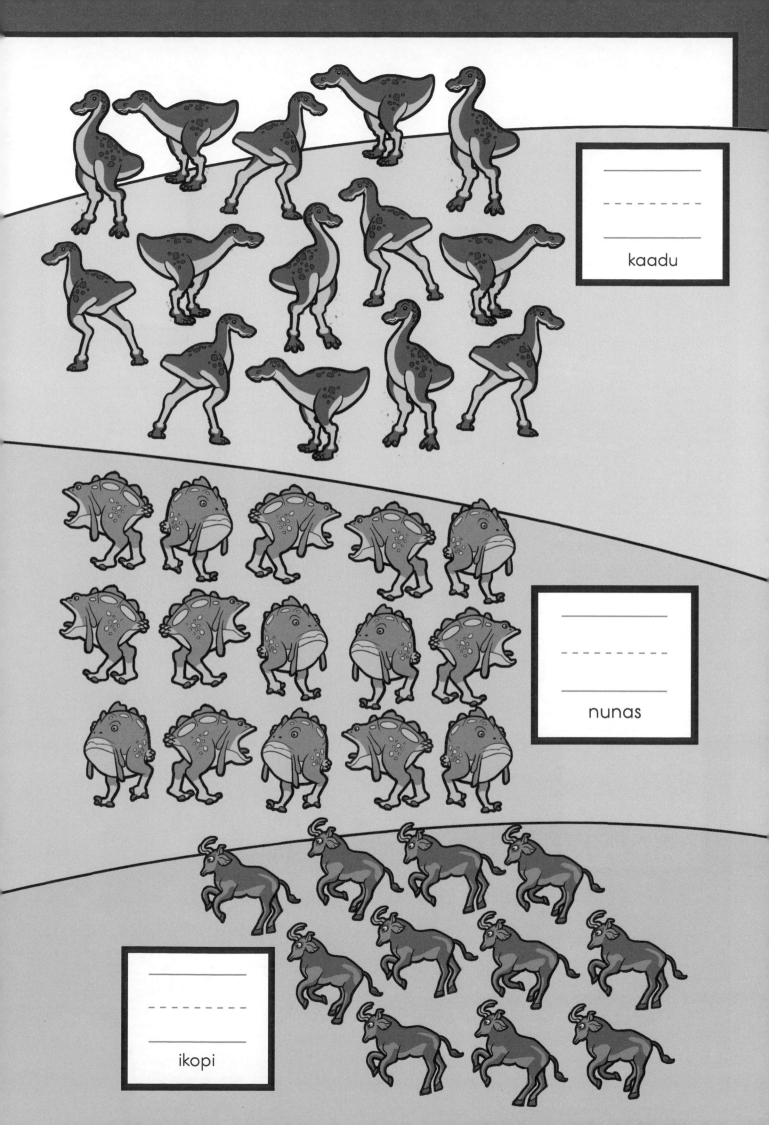

kaadu

nunas

ikopi

Space!

Count the objects in each group.

Write the number on the card next to each group.

X-wing starfighters

TIE fighters

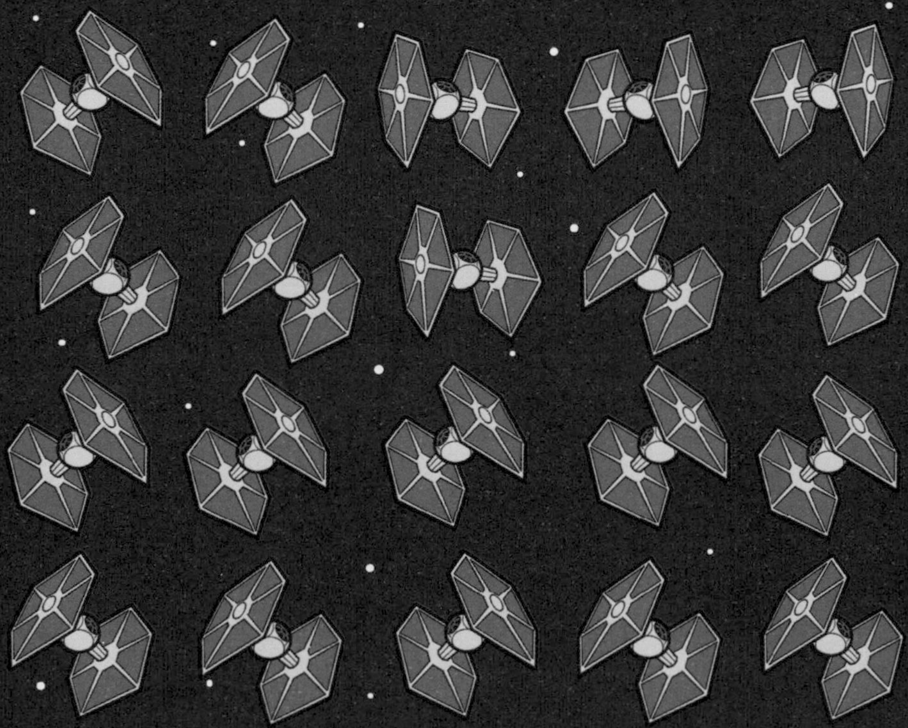

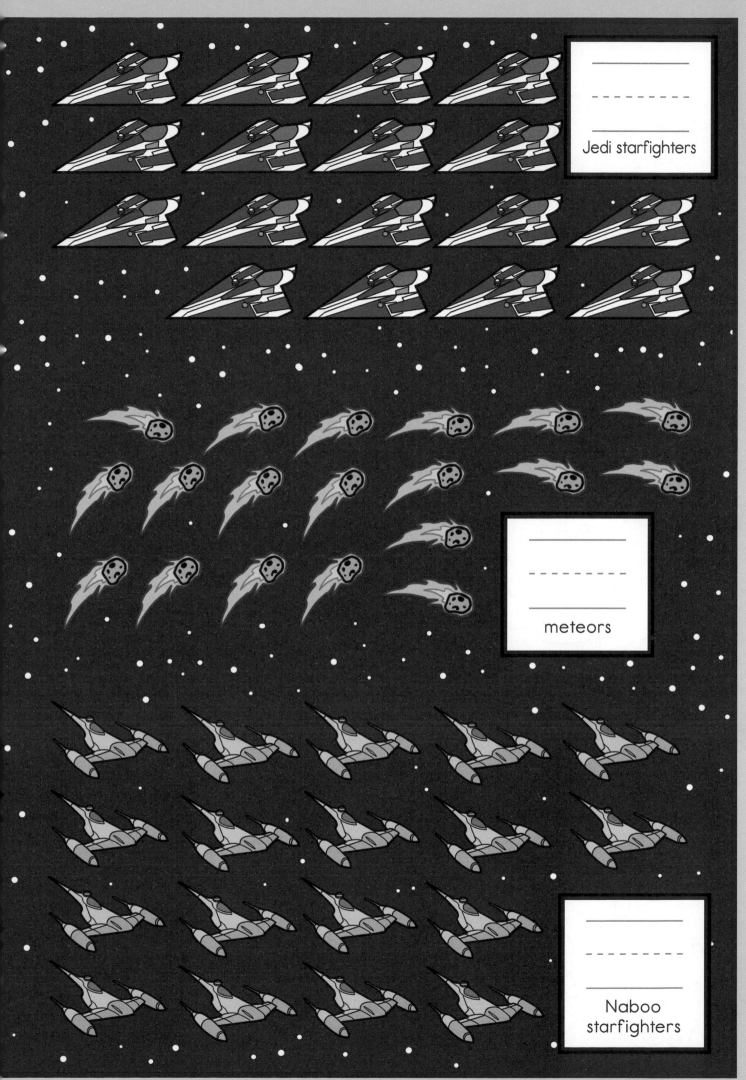

Jedi starfighters

meteors

Naboo
starfighters

Junkyard!

Help count the Jawas' junk!

Colour the  blue. _____

How many blue are there? _____

Colour the pink. _____

How many pink are there? _____

Colour the 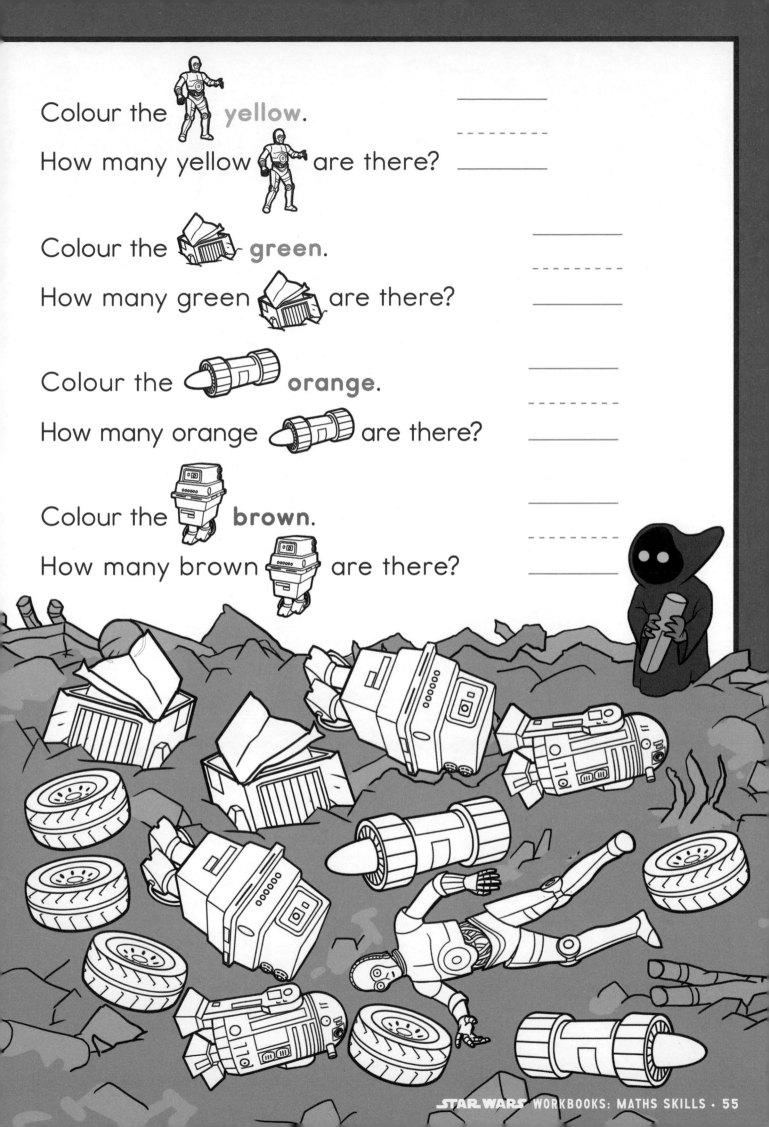 yellow. _____

How many yellow are there? _____

Colour the green. _____

How many green are there? _____

Colour the orange. _____

How many orange are there? _____

Colour the brown. _____

How many brown are there? _____

Space Jam!

Count how many you see of each starship.

Write the number on the line.

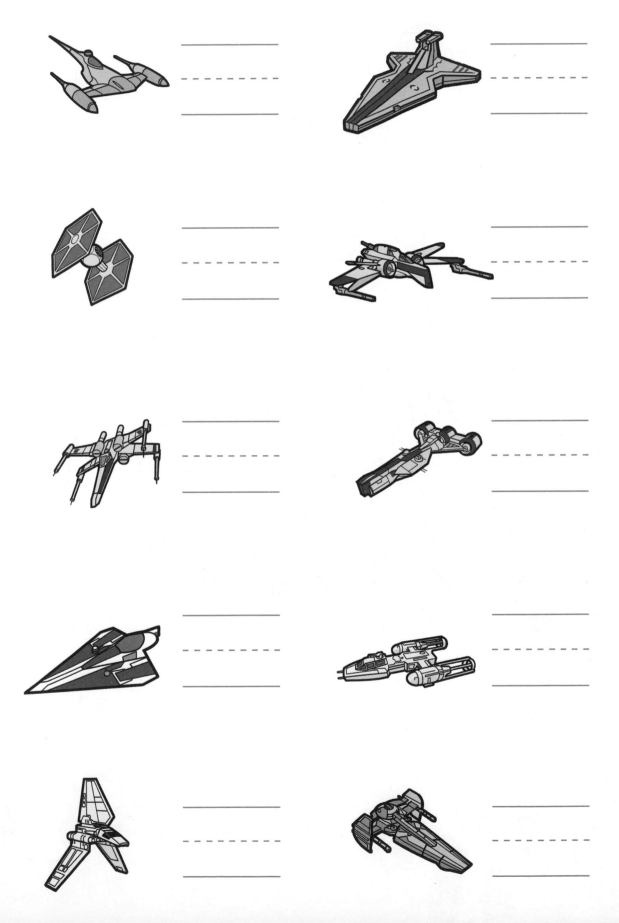

Tatooine!

What do you see on the planet Tatooine?

Count what you see!

Write the number on the line.

Troopers!

How many troopers are in each group?

Draw a line to the correct number.

11

12

13

14

15

Droids!

How many droids are in each group?

Draw a line to the correct number.

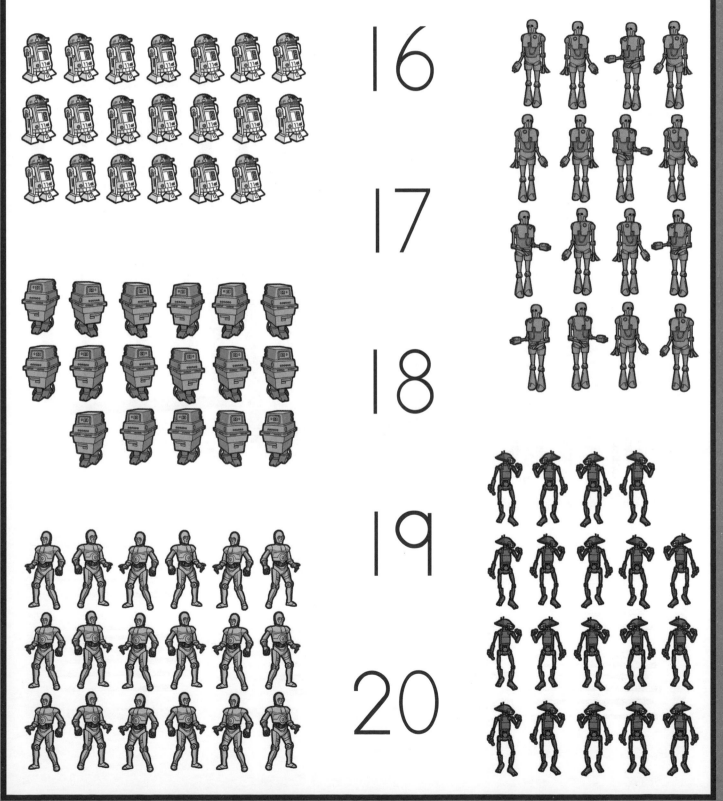

16

17

18

19

20

More

Count the lightsabers on each pair of cards.

Colour in the card that has **more** lightsabers.
Ask an adult for help if you get stuck.

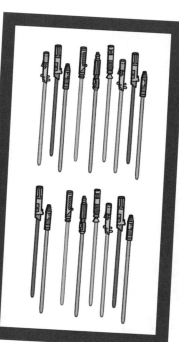

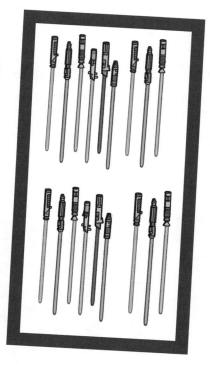

Fewer

Count the lightsabers on each pair of cards.

Colour in the card that has **fewer** lightsabers.
Ask an adult for help if you get stuck.

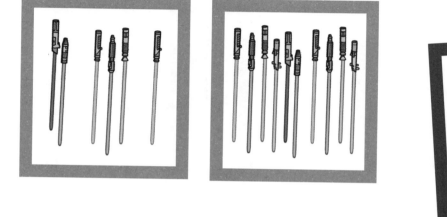

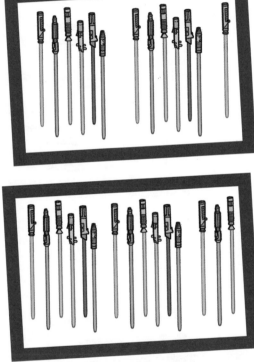

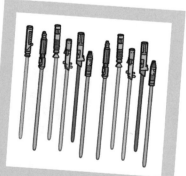

Equal

Count the lightsabers on each set of three cards.

Circle the two cards in each set that have the same, or equal, number of lightsabers.

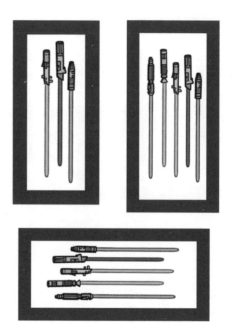

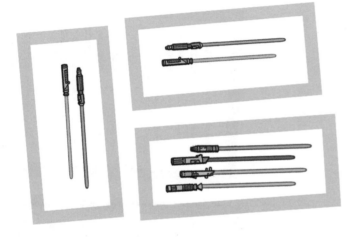

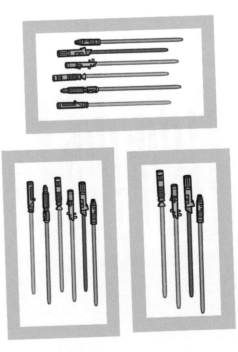

More Jawas

Count the Jawas in each group.

Circle the group that has **more** Jawas.

Ewok Addition!

You **add** to find out how many things there are all together.

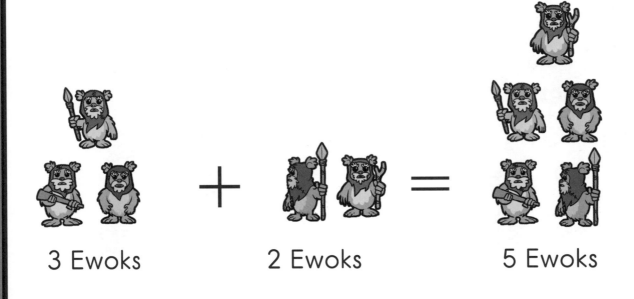

3 Ewoks   2 Ewoks   5 Ewoks

Here's how that looks as a number sentence:

$$3 + 2 = 5$$

Write the number sentence for each group.

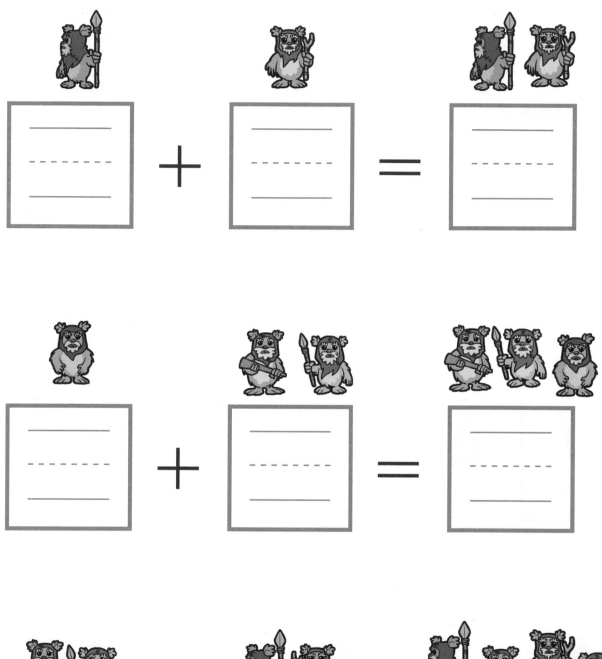

Obi-Wan Adds!

Count the objects in each group.

Write the number sentence for each group.

$$2 + 3 = 5$$

$$\_\_ + \_\_ = \_\_$$

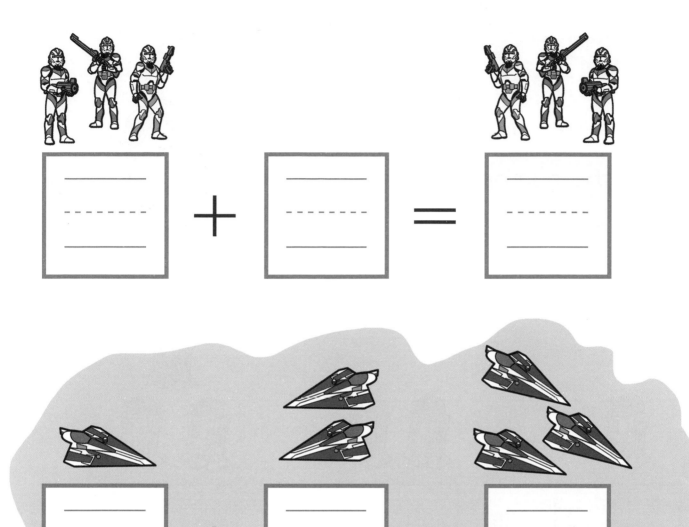

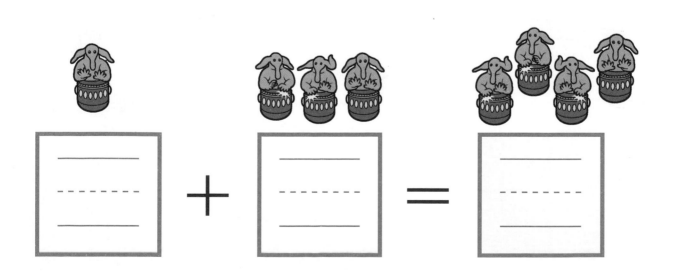

Anakin Adds!

Count the objects in each group.

Write the number sentence for each group.

[____] + [____] = [____]

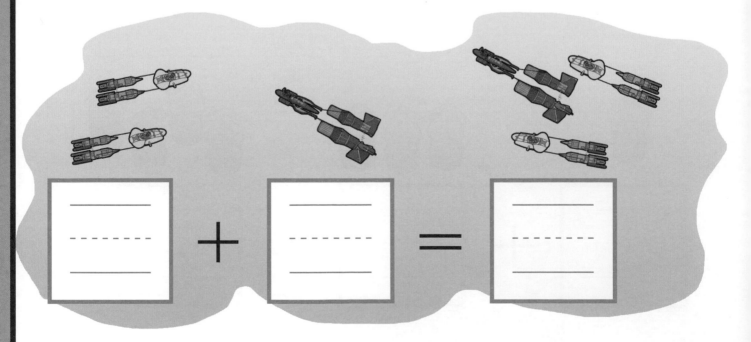

[____] + [____] = [____]

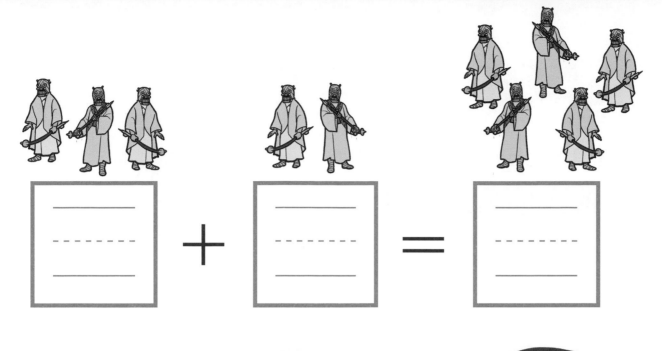

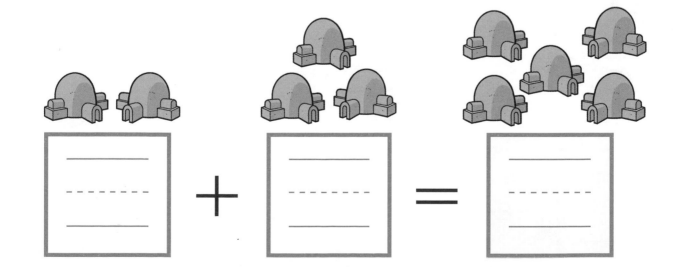

Luke Adds!

Count the objects in each group.

Write the number sentence.

Write the **sum** in the yellow box.

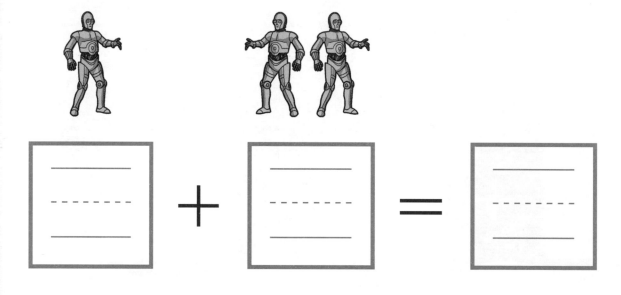

$$\boxed{} + \boxed{} = \boxed{}$$

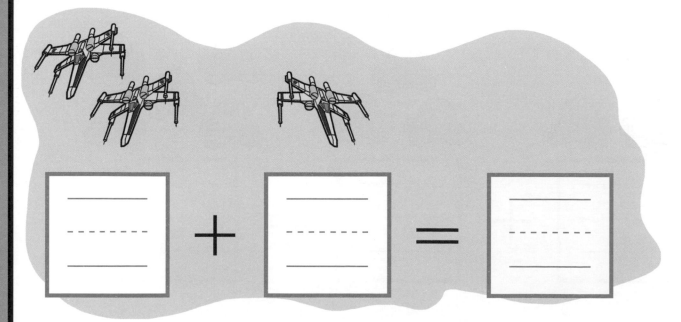

$$\boxed{} + \boxed{} = \boxed{}$$

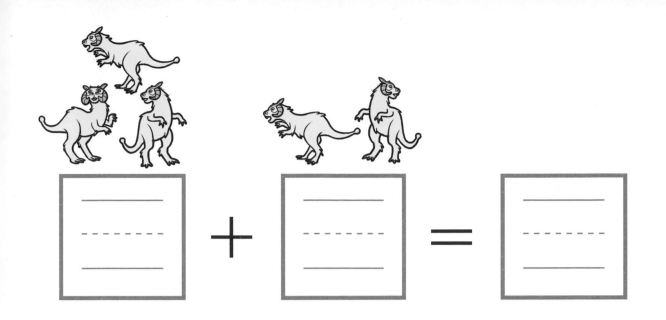

☐ + ☐ = ☐

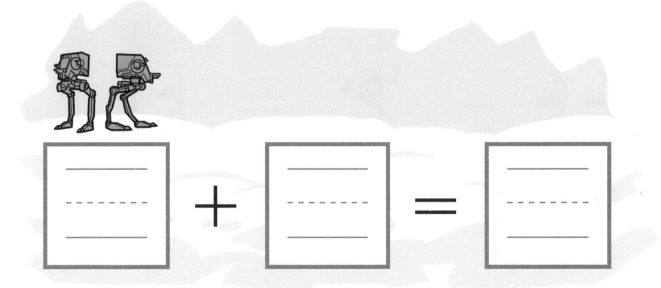

☐ + ☐ = ☐

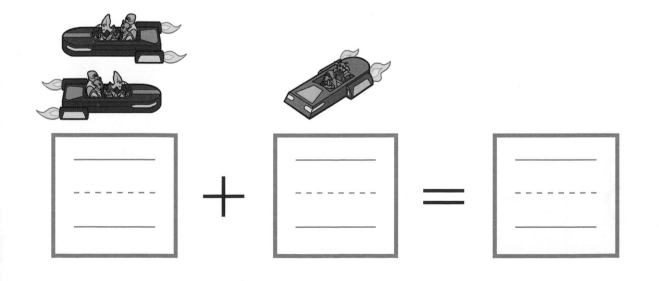

☐ + ☐ = ☐

Droid Subtraction!

To **subtract** you take away.

3 droids   1 droid   2 droids

Here's how that looks as a number sentence:

$$3 - 1 = 2$$

Write the number sentence for each group.

Row 1:
$$\boxed{} - \boxed{} = \boxed{}$$

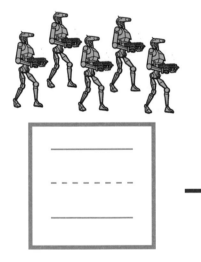  

Row 2:
$$\boxed{} - \boxed{} = \boxed{}$$

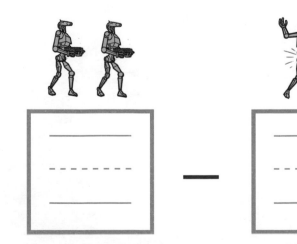  

Row 3:
$$\boxed{} - \boxed{} = \boxed{}$$

Leia Subtracts!

Count the objects in each group.

Write the number sentence for each group.

$$4 - 2 = 2$$

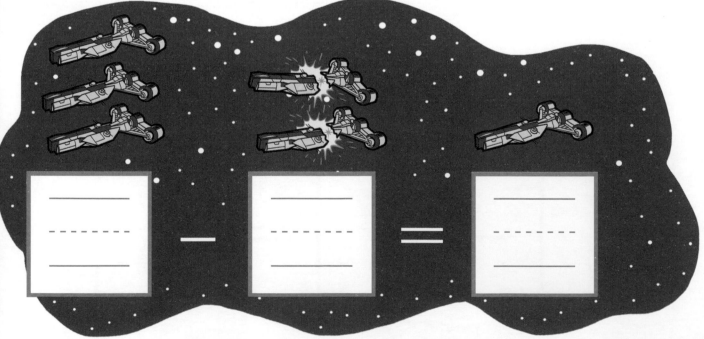

Darth Vader Subtracts!

Count the objects in each group.

Write the number sentence for each group.

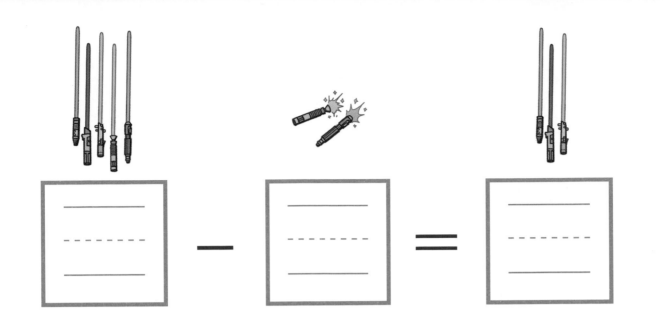

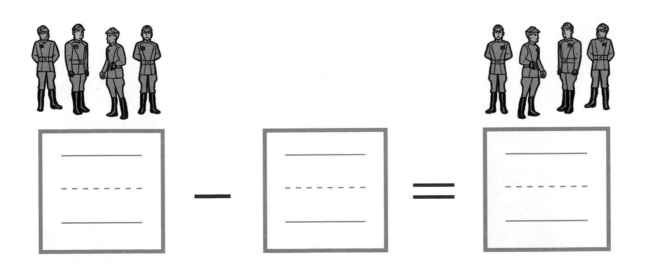

Count Dooku Subtracts!

Count the objects in each group.

Write the number sentence.

Write the **difference** in the yellow box.

Ask an adult for help if you get stuck.

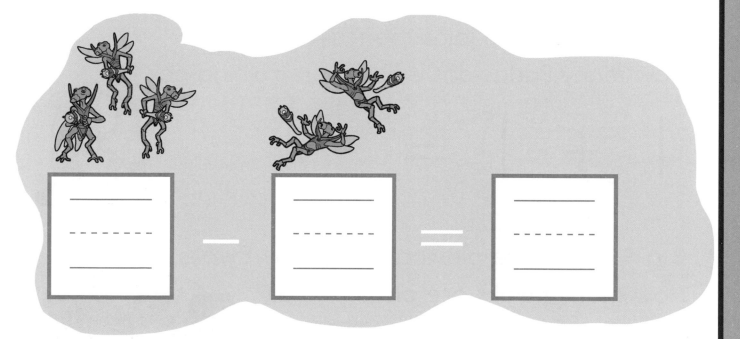

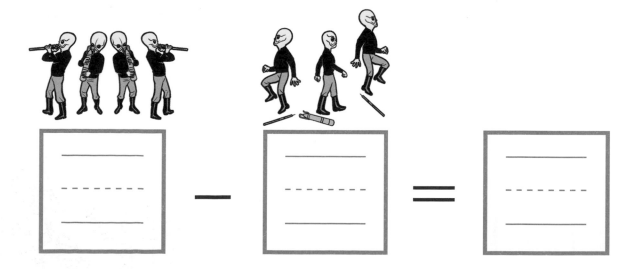

Qui-Gon Adds!

Read the addition word problems.

Write the **sum** in the yellow box.

Use the pictures to help you.

Qui-Gon is training **1** Padawan.
1 more Padawan joins the training.
How many Padawans is Qui-Gon training now?

$$1 + 1 =$$

2 girl Ewoks are playing with **2** boy Ewoks.
How many Ewoks are playing in all?

$$2 + 2 =$$

Qui-Gon is fighting **2** battle droids.
1 more battle droid joins the fight.
How many battle droids is Qui-Gon fighting now?

$$2 + 1 =$$

Yoda Subtracts!

Read the subtraction word problems.

Write the difference in the yellow box.

Use the pictures to help you.

Yoda holds 2 lightsabers. He gives 1 to Luke.
How many lightsabers is Yoda holding now?

$$2 - 1 =$$

4 TIE fighters are flying through space.
2 of them are shot down.
How many TIE fighters are flying now?

$$4 - 2 =$$

Yoda uses the Force to make 3 rocks float.
He drops 2 of them.
How many rocks are floating now?

$$3 - 2 =$$

Starfighters

4 starfighters need to land on 2 platforms.

Help land the starfighters on the platforms in as many ways as possible.

Complete all of the number sentences.

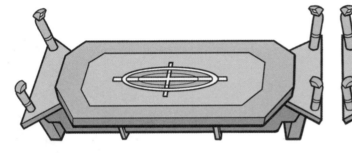

$4 = $ ☐ $ + $ ☐

$4 = $ ☐ $ + $ ☐

$4 = $ ☐ $ + $ ☐

$4 = $ ☐ $ + $ ☐

$4 = $ ☐ $ + $ ☐

Trooper Teams

5 stormtroopers need to get into 2 landspeeders.

Group the stormtroopers in as many ways as possible.

Complete all of the number sentences.

$5 = \boxed{} + \boxed{}$

$5 = \boxed{} + \boxed{}$

$5 = \boxed{} + \boxed{}$

$5 = \boxed{} + \boxed{}$

$5 = \boxed{} + \boxed{}$

$5 = \boxed{} + \boxed{}$

Lightsaber Sorting

Mace Windu needs to put 10 lightsabers into 2 boxes.

Group the lightsabers in as many ways as possible.

Complete all of the number sentences.

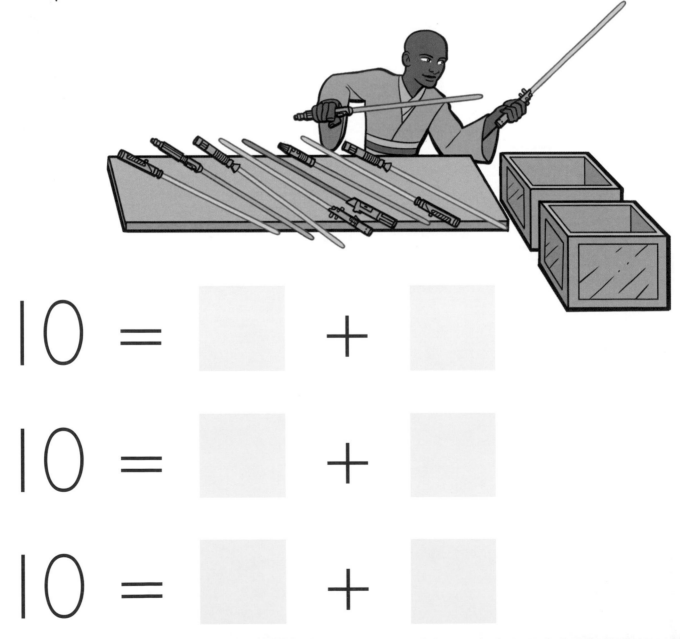

10 = ☐ + ☐

10 = ☐ + ☐

10 = ☐ + ☐

10 = ▢ + ▢

10 = ▢ + ▢

10 = ▢ + ▢

10 = ▢ + ▢

10 = ▢ + ▢

10 = ▢ + ▢

10 = ▢ + ▢

10 = ▢ + ▢

C-3PO Adds and Subtracts!

Add or **subtract** the numbers.

Write the answers in the yellow boxes.

Ask an adult for help if you get stuck.

$$4 + 1 = \boxed{}$$

$$3 + 2 = \boxed{}$$

$$1 + 1 = \boxed{}$$

$$5 - 3 = \boxed{}$$

$$4 - 1 =$$

$$3 - 2 =$$

$$1 + 3 =$$

$$2 + 2 =$$

$$3 - 1 =$$

$$4 - 3 =$$

Yoda Counts!

Help Yoda count to 100.

Fill in the missing numbers

Ask an adult for help if you get stuck.

1	2			5			8		10
	12		14	15		17		19	
		23	24			27	28		30
31	32				36			39	
	42	43		45			48	49	
51			54		56		58		
61				65				69	70
		73			76	77		79	
81		83		85		87	88		
		93	94		96	97		99	

Answers

Answers

7 — pages 18–19

Trace the number 7.

Now write the number 7.

Help Anakin Skywalker win this race!
Follow the number 7 from Start to End.

8 — pages 20–21

... number 8 on his favourite clay pots.
Circle the clay pots with the number 8.

Trace the number 8.

Now write the number 8.

9 — pages 22–23

Trace the number 9.

Now write the number 9.

Help the Ewok climb the tree.
Follow the number 9 from Start to End.

10 — pages 24–25

Trace the number 10.

Now write the number 10.

What are Darth Maul and
Emperor Palpatine looking at?
Colour in the spaces with the number 10.

11 — pages 26–27

... lot of numbers at the market.
Circle each number 11.

Trace the number 11.

Now write the number 11.

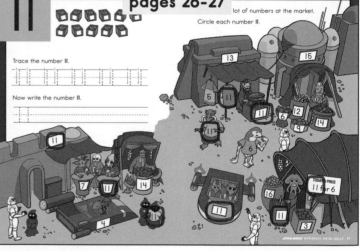

12 — pages 28–29

... run across the planet Hoth!
Follow the number 12 from
Start to End.

Trace the number 12.

Now write the number 12.

13 — pages 30–31

... find the tools he dropped.
Circle the tools with the number 13.

Trace the number 13.

Now write the number 13.

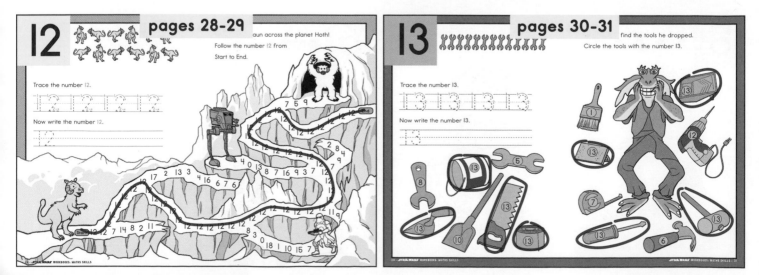

14

...find his missing parts.
Circle the parts with the number 14.

Trace the number 14.

Now write the number 14.

15

Trace the number 15.

Now write the number 15.

Help Obi-Wan Kenobi find a path through the battle droids to rescue Queen Amidala!
Follow the number 15 from Start to End.

16

...any numbers in Cloud City.
Colour in the buildings with the number 16.

Trace the number 16.

Now write the number 16.

17

Trace the number 17.

Now write the number 17.

Help Boba Fett put Han Solo into his cargo hold.
Follow the number 17 from Start to End.

18

...use the Force to make objects with the number 18 float.
Circle the objects with the number 18.

Trace the number 18.

Now write the number 18.

19

...n Amidala talking to?
Colour in the spaces with the number 19.

Trace the number 19.

Now write the number 19.

20

Trace the number 20.

Now write the number 20.

Help the ship reach the underwater city.
Follow the number 20 from Start to End.

Juggle!
How many balls is Chewbacca juggling?
Draw a line to the correct number.

Starships!
How many Jedi starfighters are in each group?
Draw a line to the correct number.

Answers

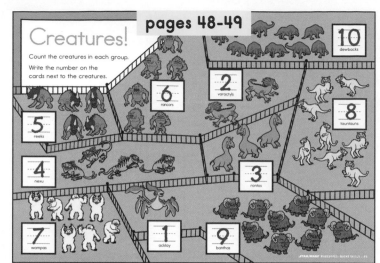

Creatures!

Count the creatures in each group.

Write the number on the cards next to the creatures.

- **10** dewbacks
- **6** rancors
- **2** varactyls
- **5** reeks
- **8** tauntauns
- **4** nexu
- **3** rontos
- **7** wampas
- **1** acklay
- **9** banthas

Visit Naboo!

Count how many creatures are in each group.

Write the number on the cards next to the creatures.

- **14** kaadu
- **13** falumpasets
- **15** nunas
- **12** shaaks
- **11** ikopi

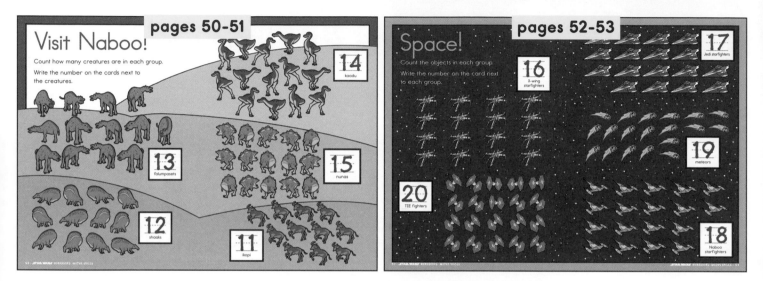

Space!

Count the objects in each group.

Write the number on the card next to each group.

- **16** X-wing starfighters
- **17** Jedi starfighters
- **20** TIE fighters
- **19** meteors
- **18** Naboo starfighters

Junkyard!

Help count the Jawas' junk!

Colour the blue. How many blue are there? **5**

Colour the pink. How many pink are there? **10**

Colour the yellow. How many yellow are there? **2**

Colour the green. How many green are there? **4**

Colour the orange. How many orange are there? **7**

Colour the brown. How many brown are there? **3**

Space Jam!

Count how many you see of each starship.

Write the number on the line.

- **6**
- **1**
- **10**
- **5**
- **8**
- **4**
- **7**
- **2**
- **9**
- **3**

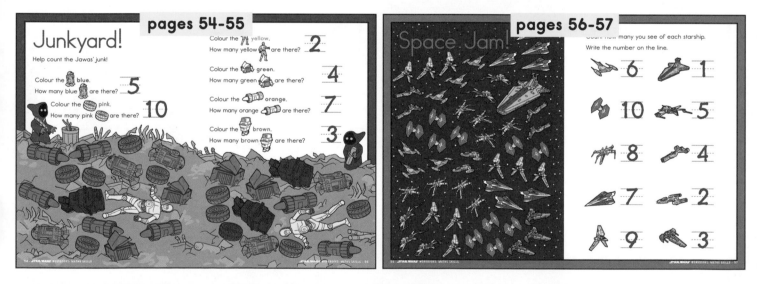

Tatooine!

What do you see on the planet Tatooine?

Count what you see!

Write the number on the line.

- **7**
- **13**
- **12**
- **11**
- **8**
- **5**
- **2**
- **4**

Troopers!

How many troopers are in each group?

Draw a line to the correct number.

- 11
- 12
- 13
- 14
- 15

Droids!

How many droids are in each group?

Draw a line to the correct number.

- 16
- 17
- 18
- 19
- 20

More

Count the lightsabers on each pair of cards.

Colour in the card that has **more** lightsabers. Ask an adult for help if you get stuck.

Fewer

Count the lightsabers on each pair of cards.

Colour in the card that has **fewer** lightsabers. Ask an adult for help if you get stuck.

Equal

Count the lightsabers on each set of three cards.

Circle the two cards in each set that have the same, or **equal**, number of lightsabers.

More Jawas

Count the Jawas in each group.

Circle the group that has **more** Jawas.

Ewok Addition!

You **add** to find out how many things there are all together.

3 Ewoks + 2 Ewoks = 5 Ewoks

Here's how that looks as a number sentence:

$3 + 2 = 5$

...number sentence for each group.

$1 + 1 = 2$

$1 + 2 = 3$

$2 + 2 = 4$

Obi-Wan Adds!

Count the objects in each group.

Write the number sentence for each group.

$3 + 0 = 3$

$2 + 3 = 5$

$1 + 2 = 3$

$1 + 1 = 2$

$1 + 3 = 4$

Anakin Adds!

Count the objects in each group.

Write the number sentence for each group.

$3 + 2 = 5$

$1 + 2 = 3$

$1 + 4 = 5$

$2 + 1 = 3$

$2 + 3 = 5$

Luke Adds!

Count the objects in each group.

Write the number sentence.

Write the **sum** in the yellow box.

$3 + 2 = 5$

$1 + 2 = 3$

$2 + 0 = 2$

$2 + 1 = 3$

$2 + 1 = 3$

Droid Subtraction!

To **subtract** you take away.

3 droids − 1 droid = 2 droids

Here's how that looks as a number sentence:

$3 - 1 = 2$

...number sentence for each group.

$4 - 2 = 2$

$5 - 2 = 3$

$2 - 1 = 1$

Leia Subtracts!

Count the objects in each group.

Write the number sentence for each group.

$3 - 1 = 2$

$4 - 2 = 2$

$5 - 4 = 1$

$3 - 2 = 1$

$3 - 2 = 1$

Answers

pages 78-79

Darth Vader Subtracts!

Count the objects in each group.

Write the number sentence for each group.

$5 - 2 = 3$

$4 - 2 = 2$

$3 - 2 = 1$

$2 - 1 = 1$

$4 - 0 = 4$

pages 80-81

Count Dooku Subtracts!

Count the objects in each group.

Write the number sentence.

Write the difference in the yellow box.

Ask an adult for help if you get stuck.

$5 - 0 = 5$

$4 - 2 = 2$

$3 - 2 = 1$

$3 - 1 = 2$

$4 - 3 = 1$

pages 82-83

Qui-Gon Aaas!

Read the addition word problems.

Write the sum in the yellow box.

Use the pictures to help you.

Qui-Gon is training 1 Padawan.
1 more Padawan joins the training.
How many Padawans is Qui-Gon training now?

$1 + 1 = 2$

2 girl Ewoks are playing with 2 boy Ewoks.
How many Ewoks are playing in all?

$2 + 2 = 4$

Qui-Gon is fighting 2 battle droids.
1 more battle droid joins the fight.
How many battle droids is Qui-Gon fighting now?

$2 + 1 = 3$

Yoda Subtracts!

Read the subtraction word problems.

Write the difference in the yellow box.

Use the pictures to help you.

Yoda holds 2 lightsabers. He gives 1 to Luke.
How many lightsabers is Yoda holding now?

$2 - 1 = 1$

4 TIE fighters are flying through space.
2 of them are shot down.
How many TIE fighters are flying now?

$4 - 2 = 2$

Yoda uses the Force to make 3 rocks float.
He drops 2 of them.
How many rocks are floating now?

$3 - 2 = 1$

pages 84-85

Starfighters

4 starfighters need to land on 2 platforms.

Help land the starfighters on the platforms in as many ways as possible.

Complete all of the number sentences.

$4 = 4 + 0$
$4 = 3 + 1$
$4 = 2 + 2$
$4 = 1 + 3$
$4 = 0 + 4$

Trooper Teams

5 stormtroopers need to get into 2 landspeeders.

Group the stormtroopers in as many ways as possible.

Complete all of the number sentences.

$5 = 5 + 0$
$5 = 4 + 1$
$5 = 3 + 2$
$5 = 2 + 3$
$5 = 1 + 4$
$5 = 0 + 5$

pages 86-87

Lightsaber Sorting

Mace Windu needs to put 10 lightsabers into 2 boxes.

Group the lightsabers in as many ways as possible.

Complete all of the number sentences.

$10 = 10 + 0$
$10 = 9 + 1$
$10 = 8 + 2$
$10 = 7 + 3$
$10 = 6 + 4$
$10 = 5 + 5$
$10 = 4 + 6$
$10 = 3 + 7$
$10 = 2 + 8$
$10 = 1 + 9$
$10 = 0 + 10$

pages 88-89

C-3PO Aaas and Subtracts!

Add or subtract the numbers.

Write the answers in the yellow boxes.

Ask an adult for help if you get stuck.

$4 + 1 = 5$

$3 + 2 = 5$

$1 + 1 = 2$

$5 - 3 = 2$

$4 - 1 = 3$

$3 - 2 = 1$

$1 + 3 = 4$

$2 + 2 = 4$

$3 - 1 = 2$

$4 - 3 = 1$

page 90

Yoda Counts!

Help Yoda count to 100.

Fill in the missing numbers.

Ask an adult for help if you get stuck.

1	2	3	4	5	6	7	8	9	10
11	12	13	14	15	16	17	18	19	20
21	22	23	24	25	26	27	28	29	30
31	32	33	34	35	36	37	38	39	40
41	42	43	44	45	46	47	48	49	50
51	52	53	54	55	56	57	58	59	60
61	62	63	64	65	66	67	68	69	70
71	72	73	74	75	76	77	78	79	80
81	82	83	84	85	86	87	88	89	90
91	92	93	94	95	96	97	98	99	100